Angela Parker Jones

Raleigh, NC 27616

Coachangelapjones@gmail.com

HAVE A HEALTHY LIFESTYLE BY

EATING ALKALINE FOODS

by

Angela Parker Jones

Throw the Junk Out

I want to thank you for taking the first step on wanting to have a healthy Transformation. Eating healthy and plant-based foods is a great medicine for your body, it is going to take discipline and dedication. You got to want it, stay positive, and DON'T GIVE UP!!! So, what are you going to do to make the change? If you do not know I can help...

We will start by looking in your kitchen for the

throw away products

- ☐ Candy

- ☐ Chips

- ☐ Processed Foods

- ☐ Soft Drinks

- ☐ Canned Fruit

- ☐ Alcohol

- ☐ Margarine

- ☐ Chocolate

- ☐ Oatmeal

- ☐ Dairy (creams, yogurt, hard cheese, ice cream)

- ☐ Bacon

- ☐ Coffee

- ☐ Beef

- ☐ Pork

- ☐ Pies

- ☐ Roasted Nuts

- ☐ White Potatoes

- ☐ Citrus Fruits (oranges)

- ☐ Fried food

- ☐ Grains

- ☐ Other of foods and drinks not listed that is keeping you from achieve your goal. For example, packaged and processed foods with sodium and sugar.

Now that was not so bad was it! These are the foods that could be holding you back on achieving your healthy goals.

What drinks to avoid

Caffeinated drinks-

- Soda

- Coffee with added creams and sugar

- Energy drinks

- Alcohol

- Tea with added sugar

- Pre- bottled Smoothie

What type of water are you drinking?

In this transformation journey we will focus on drinking alkaline water. Alkaline water has a high pH level for your body when having an Alkaline Food Lifestyle. If you do not have alkaline water you can add lemon, lime, or pH drops to your water. It will change your water to alkaline water.

I want to give you basic information on

how to drink water to lose weight

(Weight)	(Water)	(Water Bottle)
☐ 80lbs	40oz	2
☐ 100lbs	50oz	3
☐ 120lbs	60oz	4
☐ 140lbs	70oz	4
☐ 160lbs	80oz	5
☐ 180lbs	90oz	5
☐ 200lbs	100oz	6
☐ 220lbs	110oz	6
☐ 240lbs	120oz	7
☐ 260lbs	130oz	7
☐ 280lbs	140oz	8
☐ 300lbs	150oz	8
☐ 300lbs	160oz	9
☐ 320lbs	170oz	10

Let us Fuel the Body with Alkaline Foods

When picking your foods look for the labels that say organic. Foods to look for are as follows

☐ Spinach

☐ Asparagus

☐ Cucumbers

☐ Seeded Watermelon

☐ Broccoli

☐ Bell Peppers

☐ Garlic

☐ Raisins

☐ Beets

☐ Fruits

☐ Kale Sprouts

☐ Zucchini

☐ Zucchini Noodles

☐ Fresh Mushrooms

☐ Tomatoes

☐ Ginger

☐ Brussel Sprouts

☐ Peppers

☐ Celery

☐ Parsley

☐ Corn

☐ Wild Rice

☐ Green Drinks

- ☐ Onions

- ☐ Sesame Seed

- ☐ Beans of any kind

- ☐ Plant Based Protein

- ☐ Cinnamon

- ☐ Curry Powder

- ☐ Almond Milk (make sure there is NO CARRAGENNAN in the ingredients. It causes bloating, cause colon cancer, inflammation, food allergies, irritable bowel syndrome. Almond milk is alkaline forming. The pH ranges from 6.5 to 7.

Smoothie/ Protein Shake

Learn to make your own smoothie/protein

shake, that way you know it is natural with

no added ingredients you do not need.

Examples of what to put in your

smoothie

1. Raw Vegetables-Spinach, Arugula,

    Kale, Romaine, they have a lot

    nutrient.

2. Water or Silk Almond Milk'

3. Berry, Apple, Bananas, mango, pine

    apple

It is Best to eat RAW VEGETABLES because high in alkaline. You can steam to keep most of the nutrients. Keep your mealtimes the same to maintain your blood sugar level. Herbs and Spices change the pH level in your body to the alkaline side. The benefit of having an alkaline state is it increases your immune system and kills bacteria. Help with weight loss. Help improve hormone level. To have a healthy lifestyle do **NOT**

SKIP MEALS. Get plenty of sleep, be physically

active, have a creative mind when creating your meals,

finally have a cut off time when eating your last meal of

the day**.**

What Kind of Exercise Are You Doing?

Before exercise avoid SUGARS AND GRAINS!!!
Yoga will be great. Yoga is great for stress and
breathing naturally detoxes your body. Help weight
loss, increase flexibility, tones your body, and good for
your soul.

What Kind of Movement are You Doing?

- ☐ Walking
- ☐ Running
- ☐ Yoga
- ☐ Pilates
- ☐ Weight Training
- ☐ Swimming
- ☐ Jump Rope
- ☐ Golf
- ☐ Skateboarding
- ☐ Zumba
- ☐ Hiking
- ☐ Rock Climbing
- ☐ Dance
- ☐ Basketball
- ☐ Cycling
- ☐ Cleaning
- ☐ Frisbee

Anyone of these can help you live a healthy lifestyle and help with weight loss. Exercise can help with more energy. It can help with releasing bacteria from your lungs and airways. Can lower your risk of getting an illness. Help boost your immune system to fight off disease. It also helps strengthen your muscles. Finally, it helps with stress.

25 DAY SIT UP CHALLENGE

Day 1 20 SIT UPS

Day 2 25 SIT UPS

Day 3 30 SIT UPS

Day 4 **REST DAY**

Day 5 35 SIT UPS

Day 6 40 SIT UPS

Day 7 45 SIT UPS

Day 8 **REST DAY**

Day 9 50 SIT UPS

Day 10 55 SIT UPS

Day 11 60 SIT UPS

Day 12 **REST DAY**

Day 13 65 SIT UPS

Day 14 70 SIT UPS

Day 15 75 SIT UPS

Day 16 **REST DAY**

Day 17 80 SIT UPS

Day 18 85 SIT UPS

Day 19 90 SIT UPS

Day 20 **REST DAY**

Day 21 95 SIT UPS

Day 22 100 SIT UPS

Day 23 105 SIT UPS

Day 22 **REST DAY**

Day 23 110 SIT UPS

Day 24 115 SIT UPS

Day 25 120 SIT UPS

20 Day SQUAT CHALLENGE

Day 1 25 Squats

Day 2 30 Squats

Day 3 35 Squats

Day 4 **REST DAY**

Day 5 40 Squats

Day 6 45 Squats

Day 7 50 Squats

Day 8 **REST DAY**

Day 9 55 Squats

Day 10 60 Squats

Day 11 65 Squats

Day 12 **REST DAY**

Day 13 70 Squats

Day 14 75 Squats

Day 15 80 Squats

Day 16 **REST DAY**

Day 17 85 Squats

Day 18 90 Squats

Day 19 95 Squats

Day 20 100 Squats

YouTube Channel

Angela Parker Jones

Herbal Teas

- **Green Tea**- Help with weight loss. Reason for that the extract can boost your metabolism to help the body burn fat. Can help to prevent **diabetes**. Can be used to control blood sugar and slow the progression. Green Tea is healthy for your skin. great **Antioxidant**. Best time to drink Green Tea is early morning or lunch. Drink at least one to two cups a day.

- **Peppermint Herbal Tea-** Reduces Stress, treats bad breath, improves digestion, can reduce pain, improve immune system, burn fat, reduces fever, and promotes healthy skin and hair.

- **Apple Ginger Green Tea -**Help with weight loss and reduce belly fat, help cut calories

- **Chamomile Tea-**Help treat cold symptoms, help with sleep, relaxation, help reduce menstrual pain, help treat diabetes and lower blood sugar and help reduce inflammation.

- **Black Tea-**Antioxidants help to have healthy bones and help with stress relief.

- **Lemongrass Tea-**Lower cholesterol. Antioxidant, may help with weight loss, help with bloating, menstrual cramps, and hot flashes.

Brussel Sprouts-Alkaline

Boiling or cooking the sprouts does kill some nutrients

and vitamins. You can enjoy, raw or boiled. Brussel

Sprouts are high in protein, rich in fiber, vitamin c,

contain different minerals and iron. May help maintain

healthy blood sugar levels. Brussel sprouts are rich in

vitamin k.

- Vitamin C-Help with iron absorption

- High Fiber- Help Improve Blood Sugar Control. Increases your bowel frequency and soften your stool.

- Rich in Vitamin K- May help with Osteoporosis.

- Antioxidants-May help lower risk of chronic disease.

Alkaline Breakfast RECIPES
Alkaline Smoothie

Prep Time 10mins
Blend time 5 mins
- ☐ 2cups Kale or spinach

- ☐ 1 cup of Organic protein powder

- ☐ 1Tablespoon Flaxseed or Chia Seed

- ☐ Water or Silk Milk

- ☐ ½ cup of berries

- ☐ 3-4 packs of stevia sugar

1. Add all ingredients in blender. Add Ice
2. Blend on high speed for 5mins
3. Ready to Serve

Alkaline Salad 1

Prep Time-15 mins

Serving 1-2

Ingredients

- ☐ 2 cups Kale

- ☐ ½ Cup Onion, chopped

- ☐ 1 Zucchini, chopped

- ☐ 1 Squash, chopped

- ☐ 1 Bag of Peppers, chopped

- ☐ Apple Cider Vinegar

- ☐ 3 Tomatoes, chopped

- ☐ 2 Tablespoon of Italian Season

- ☐ 1 Lemon, squeeze

  1. Mixed All Ingredients

  2. Ready to serve

Alkaline Salad 2

Prep Time 15 mins

Serving 1-2

Ingredients-

- ☐ 2 Cups of Kale
- ☐ 1 Cup Cucumber Spiral
- ☐ 1 Cup Chopped Onion
- ☐ 1 Tablespoon of Italian Herbs
- ☐ ½ Cup Apple Cider Vinegar
- ☐ ½ Cup Carrots, chopped
- ☐ 2 Tomatoes, chopped
- ☐ ¼ Cup dry roasted, unsalted Almonds

1. Mix all ingredients together
2. Ready to serve

Alkaline Vegetable Soup
Prep Time 20 mins
Serving 2-5
Ingredients

- ☐ 2 Cabbage, Chopped

- ☐ 2 Stalked Celery, Chopped

- ☐ 2-3 Tablespoon Garlic Minced

- ☐ 2 Tablespoon Olive

- ☐ 2 Onions, Chopped

- ☐ 3 Whole Tomatoes, Chopped

- ☐ 2 Tablespoon Basil

- ☐ 4 Bay Leaves

- ☐ 2- 4 Cups of Peppers, Chopped

- ☐ 2-3, Chopped

- ☐ 2-3 Zucchini, Chopped

- ☐ 2-3 Cups of Corn

- ☐ 1Cup or 32oz Organic Vegetable Broth
`

Directions

1. In a large pot over medium heat, heat olive oil.

2. Add all the ingredients.

3. Stir often until vegetables are soft for 20mins.

4. Simmer for 10mins

5. Remove from heat and serve.

Stuffed Peppers

Prep Time 20 mins
Serving 3-5

Ingredients

☐ 7 Large Peppers

- ☐ Ground Turkey Meat

- ☐ 1-2 Large Onion (chopped)

- ☐ 1-2 Large Tomatoes (chopped)

- ☐ 1 Teaspoon Italian Herbs

- ☐ 1 Teaspoon Basil Herbs

- ☐ Pinch of Shredded Cheese of your choice

- ☐ 1 Tomato Paste 6oz. can

- ☐ 3-4 Organic Mini Sweet Peppers (chopped)

Directions

1. Cut Stem off each Large pepper. Remove all seeds and membranes.

2. Rinse Large Peppers

3. Heat Oven 350 F

4. Cook Ground Turkey over stove in a medium to large pan

5. Stuff Peppers with all the ingredients except the cheese

6. Cook in oven until peppers are tender.

7. Add cheese for about 1-2 mins

8. Finally, you may serve

Tracking Your Progress

Helps you stay focused on what

is **important** to why you are trying to

reach **your** goal. Take **before** and **after**

pictures of yourself.

Tracking help you to stay POSITIVE.

REWARD yourself when Achieving your

goals…

Do not compare your path with anybody else's.

Your path is Your unique path.

Veggie Noodles

1. Boil 15 mins

2. Serve with any side you choose

Squash

Peppers

Onions

Zucchini

Herbs

Healthy Tips:

Healthy Carbohydrates is made up of carbon,

hydrogen, and oxygen. Carbohydrates is

produced from plants.

Non-Starchy Carbs, Unlimited Servings

1. Herbs

2. Onions

3. Bean Sprouts

4. Celery

5. Cucumber

6. Green Beans

7. Ginger Root

8. Snap Beans

9. Bell Peppers

10. Lettuce

11. Brussels Sprouts

12. Cauliflower

13. Eggplant

14. Spinach

15. Tomatoes

16. Zucchini

17. Garlic

18. Kale

19. Cabbage

20. Arugula

BE

CONSISTENT

YOU WILL

FINISH

STRONG!!!

Transformation... Feel Great about YOURSELF no matter what size you are. It is about FEELING great and having a HEALTHY lifestyle.

Check with your physician before you make any changes if you have health issues or are taking medication.

Do not Stress yourself on how much weight you lose, it is about being healthy. Love Yourself and Stay Stress Free.

Start Pointing Out What You Love About Yourself Rather Than What You Hate

Keep in Mind

Healthy Diet

Regular Exercise

Relax

Get Plenty of Rest

Are you willing to fight for yourself?

BE Honest with yourself and set realistic

goals.

You will get great results and you will be

proud of yourself. Like I said earlier in the

book THROW OUT THE JUNK!!! What

ever is stopping you from getting your

results of what you want for yourself.

FIGHT FIGHT FIGHT, FOR YOURSELF.

YOU ARE WORTH FIGHTING FOR.

I want to dedicate this book to my Applewhite,
Parker, and Jones family… I love you!!!
Special dedication to Chloe', Mason, and Ke'Mari

Made in the USA
Columbia, SC
15 January 2021